NIGHT UNTO NIGHT

ALSO BY MARTHA COLLINS

POETRY

Admit One: An American Scrapbook
Day Unto Day
White Papers
Blue Front
Some Things Words Can Do
A History of Small Life on a Windy Planet
The Arrangement of Space
The Catastrophe of Rainbows

POETRY CHAPBOOKS
Sheer
Gone So Far

TRANSLATIONS

Bitter and Sweet: Poems by Trang The Hy
(cotranslated with Nguyen Ba Chung)
Black Stars: Poems by Ngo Tu Lap
(cotranslated with the author)
Green Rice: Poems by Lam Thi My Da
(cotranslated with Thuy Dinh)
The Women Carry River Water: Poems by Nguyen Quang Thieu
(cotranslated with the author)

EDITED BOOKS

Into English: Poems, Translations, Commentaries
(coedited with Kevin Prufer)
Catherine Breese Davis: On the Life and Work of an American Master
(coedited with Kevin Prufer and Martin Rock)
Critical Essays on Louise Bogan

NIGHT UNTO NIGHT

Poems

MARTHA COLLINS

MILKWEED EDITIONS

Published 2018 by Milkweed Editions
Printed in Canada
Cover design based on a design by Gretchen Achilles
and typeset by Mary Austin Speaker
Cover photography © Jane Fulton Alt, *The Burn*
Author photo by Doug Macomber
18 19 20 21 22   5 4 3 2 1
First Edition

Milkweed Editions, an independent nonprofit publisher, gratefully acknowledges sustaining support from the Jerome Foundation; the Lindquist & Vennum Foundation; the McKnight Foundation; the National Endowment for the Arts; the Target Foundation; and other generous contributions from foundations, corporations, and individuals. Also, this activity is made possible by the voters of Minnesota through a Minnesota State Arts Board Operating Support grant, thanks to a legislative appropriation from the arts and cultural heritage fund, and a grant from Wells Fargo. For a full listing of Milkweed Editions supporters, please visit milkweed.org.

Library of Congress Cataloging-in-Publication Data

Names: Collins, Martha, 1940- author.
Title: Night unto night : poems / Martha Collins.
Description: First edition. | Minneapolis, Minnesota : Milkweed Editions, 2018. | Includes bibliographical references.
Identifiers: LCCN 2017039308 | ISBN 9781571314895 (pbk. : alk. paper)
Classification: LCC PS3553.O4752 A6 2018 | DDC 811/.54--dc23
LC record available at https://lccn.loc.gov/2017039308

Milkweed Editions is committed to ecological stewardship. We strive to align our book production practices with this principle, and to reduce the impact of our operations in the environment. We are a member of the Green Press Initiative, a nonprofit coalition of publishers, manufacturers, and authors working to protect the world's endangered forests and conserve natural resources. *Night Unto Night* was printed on acid-free 100% postconsumer-waste paper by Friesens Corporation.

for Theodore Space
(1938–2016)

my one my love
my Ted

CONTENTS

Day unto day uttereth speech,
and night unto night sheweth knowledge.

—Psalm 19:2

To live's a Gift, to dye's a Debt that we .
Each of us owe unto Mortality.

—PHILIP PAIN, *Daily Meditations* (1668)

NIGHT UNTO NIGHT

UP NORTH

UP NORTH

March 2010

1

Up north is where I think
      we go, ghost-trees frozen
           with mist, snow
      paving the roads, cold
as we will be, no
      roads except into
           those trees, no road.

2

On a white field, faded
      text of weeds:
           1 1 1
In the distance, in the dark
      of dense trees: little patches,
           as we will be, no
      more, of illegible snow

3

Distance, in the dark,
    disappears: all
        is close, closing
           in, *here*
      is all there
  is, there is nothing
in between, no between.

4

    As a skier down
that mountain, I thought,
      bird into
    that mist, dis-
appearing into that ___
    is all there

    ___

5

That mountain I thought
     was a cloud is covered
with snow, snow
     I thought to drift
into drips from trees, trees
     are going to work
        again, drinking in.

6

     Earth shifts
its bones, quakes open
        again, drinking in
     its own, scrawled sign
on fallen wall, <u>dead</u>
     <u>body inside</u>→ body
        bodybodybodybody

7

My friend is gone,
        body inside body
                of earth, sea
        of atoms, she is,
her husband said, in a state
        of grace and will
                be forever.

8

Waterfall sculpted
        itself into water-
                fall, using cold
to mold itself solid
        and still, as if to
                be forever
falling without ever falling.

9

Snow is turning
      itself into water,
branches once thinned
      to diagram lines have lost
            their single white sentence,
roofs are setting themselves
      free in explosions of snow.

10

      Bird tree fills
with black fruit, grackles
      empty, fill again
their branches, utter together
      their single sentence,
last word a rough creak
      of opening air.

11

If bucket comes up
        empty, fill again
                with all that is
        and there's enough
again: nothing's not
        for nothing: don't forget
                the extended wings.

12

Head as in headway or
        headlight on high-
                way, way as in
wayward or in the or on
                the, onward
        with all that is
                heading my way

13

     Rain all day,
draping my shoulders,
     heading the way
          I am going, warmed
by the rain of the all of the— why
     was I thinking
       snow?

14

     Snow person, no person, person
of broken of sorry of finishing, what
         was I thinking?
No one is shooting my bombing
       my hurting my no
     one is counting
       me out.

15

One is counting, sun
    this morning, *two*
        for gorges filling
with snowmelt where two
        have fallen, no *jumped*
    this month, not counted on, no
        three, still counting up

16

Instead of black-and-white winter
    through my window
        this morning, too
many browns to count: trees
    weeds fields earth . . .
        the skin
        of the earth

17

Through my window
        brushstroked clouds
                on blue, trees
reddened with buds, fields
                with sun, there's
        even a hint of green
                on this day for green.

18

        Last week a white oval
edged with lace, today
the pond gleams
        in sun, there's
a red-winged blackbird
        fanning his tail, and
                there, that first robin.

19

Red-winged blackbird,
          same top branch, but one
                    tree down, crow drives
him away. Do I in my tower caw
          like that, or do
                    I wait below
          for your love-call, Love?

20

Same top branch, not one
          but four, now one
                    again, my bird
          sings his insistent
song, no chittery answer
          yet but arriving crows
                    don't chase him away.

21

Back with my love
        again, my bird
            for life, this first
        spring day with its baby
green blades, why did we squabble
        about nothing when we
            are as grass?

22

            . . . are as grass
the crocuses, snowdrops, young
        coming up from under, but
not the cattle grazing the grass
that fattens them up, not us:
        without roots, we grow
            only old.

23

Without roots, we grow
          up, like daffodils braving
the rain, then down, at last
          into those ghost-
                    trees or (remember
          October?) gold
                    slipping into air.

24

          Slipping into air,
                    then into that gorge
of rushing white water, or
          bursting into crude bouquets
                    of flame: thus the young
of the world we have failed
          proclaim our failure.

25

Of my Love, without whom not,
    I do not sing enough;
for the world that we have failed
    I do not do enough:
in this season of Lent (I'd forgotten,
    mea culpa), this season
    of penance, I confess.

26

Looking for yellow spring, I found
    body: molecules particles:
        we are eaters made
        to be eaten, I dreamed—
in this season I had forgotten
    (*mea culpa*), this awoke me:
        The rest is soul.

27

Friend I loved, body and fine
    mind, is gone, her end marked
        by shining words even
as speech failed. Her chosen last
    words were *I shall give*
        you rest: is soul
    afterword, or silence after?

28

Afterward, the silence *after*
    the words: yard
        half-blue again
        with scilla, little hats
    opened into stars, her
words opened my mouth, my
    god I was that yard.

29

My red-winged bird still calls
from his tree, but now
(new today) a
chittering female answers, I
open my mouth, my door
for love, my Love for life, so
easy to frame, shut, but it's you, Love, there.

30

News today, with
one to go, as once
before, but bad
this time, death
breathing down my neck—good
thing (but still those
birds!) I was thinking *snow*.

31

Up north is where I've lived
        these days, but I have some-
                where else
        to go, my once
and future love, you, no
        one else but you, be
                home soon.

Ithaca, New York

BROKEN OPEN

BROKEN OPEN

May 2011

1

May flower baskets filled
    with Labor spilling violets blue
        inviolate hyacinths Red

Square you'd leave the basket little
    ship that brought them over
        here you'd ring the bell and run

2

changed the day marked by our Hay-
    market: named it Loyalty named
        it Law fled from Labor red

or pink cherry broken open
    blossoms pinkish apple
        buds still bound by green

3

In the woods: winter's broken
    things grayed bent taken but

        leaves freed to work
filling the blanks (my account
    is shrinking: days spent)—
        to work: taking in the light

4

. . . *will not rejoice in the death* of even
    this settled account this late
        taken down and yet I yet . . .

my 3:00 a.m. robin in *darkness*
    cannot drive out darkness sings
        for his hour, sings for the light

5

apple's opened whitened clouds
        hide the late great sky's blue

                body spirit's cover wind-
driven world shivers a little

        cold shakes its petal-thin skin all
            down to its dark roots

6

water-colored blue-lined fish filling
        the creek circling turning silver
                thrash then leaping the ladders as if

the white rush were pulling them up:
        their bodies completely need so
            driven as if spirit . . .

7

line drawn knife cut body
	broken stuff taken months
	ago, why *now* this

loss less time mind
	heart hit by what

		will not now ever—

8

Mary's month: taken by broken
	into by God this Mother's

		Day broken open
by all: is it in breaking

	that spirit flows in

		out of body—?

9

lilac knots untied, why this tightening—

> ah, toward breaking: *a broken*
> *spirit . . . sacrifice*

thin pink coins fallen:
> spent flesh on the gray
> > walk where I am walking

10

friend found her death
> in the shower, took it in

> > her hand, held
it close, little one, let it feed

> on her flesh,
> > watched it grow

11

In the night while I'm dreaming
        my dead awake, robin sings
                in the light: little

chorus of one, high on his branch,
        closing down night, notes
                for the day's labor

12

High above the herring hiding
        their silver, gulls

                circled, shrieked,
laboring like, but not—

        our drones our extended
                hungers for the kill

13

Planes named for the un-
        working, the drones: our Gnats

                and Wasps, our Eagles, our hungry
Ravens, Hawks, and Condors, our deadly

        Predators, Reapers, Dark Star
                above us, our unmanned Shadow

14

This week's litter: maples'
        tiny green planes, three

                drones killed another
dozen, intended or not, in that

        distant part of the world
                war we are playing

15

Body's war: teeth hair brain
    cells lost, parts
        attacked, at last

particles breaking through
    borders: body's destruction
        its final truce

16

wanted to think *spirit*, instead body's
    turned to breaking, not away

        from love (those lilacs
again—) but slanting

      from . . . when did I start (say
      the word) to be *old*?

17

Robin, late today, calls me out
    of a dreamed house where I turned
        page after blank page while

baby played a concerto: it's his
    world, and the bird's: I write
        you from my bed, my almost sleep

18

In the rain, tulips swoon into skirts,
    pistils risen, swollen, stamens
        turned, anthers waiting—

In my house, chaste yellow eggs, never
    to break, strain from their vase
        toward the hidden sun

19

Lilacs rust in rain, redbuds shed
    magenta confetti, make
        green hearts, risen

iris wait to open lips, lilies

    of the valley oh love
        in our bed

20

Long before dawn, robin, cardinal
    sing in my dream, contra-
        puntal lines weave

a nest for my troubles, bed
    for our reddened
        blue world

21

rain all day gray
        sky world to end
                today the preacher

shut his site his end the beginning
        of troubles and God

                said *rain* said *I will destroy*

22

friend is making his soul I'm trying
        to break my spirit open to find . . .
                soul to lose . . . pride to find . . .

soul where I began: to think

        God to think end think (no robin
                this morning) *night*

23

missing letter missing word That
    of God in us, That

        Which made us, I-am-
that-I-am, hollow inside which (I)

    am missing, abyss is That
      · Which in which soul

24

petals that pinked the garden,
    grass, *all flesh*, winged seeds
      that greened the gray: all

into that abyss, that night
    that *shall be light about me*, that
      shineth as the day

25

That year I entered a green hill as if
        it were a cave, wound up a gray

                path, up was down, out-
side in: *to kneel is to get back*

        Now to wind down: kneel
                my way out

26

planes up bombs down trucks tankers
        civilians killed street fighters
                strikes and on

the reverse: seeds down iris up
        and open: purple pale
                lavender black

27

butterfly (blue in those woods) to tornado (dozens
        struck this week): chaos is cosmic

            laughter my friend said: small
to large *(a little child) (and God said)*: determined

        circles of circles, but not—oh, chaotic
                heart—what you'd expect

28

and so into night punctured with stars,
        periods ending sentences everywhere
                nowhere *circle whose center*

. . . and there it is: where *imagination*
        loses itself . . . (child at the window):

        infinity the Infinite after all

29

Long days, past petalled beginnings,
    green fills in, replaces
        patches of sky, earth

in her summer dress surrounds
    and grounds us, center's
        where we are

30

from the Civil to all to every-
    one war or not: remember Ezra
        Hepzibah *Day is done* remember

Barbara Pat now Dave *gone*
    the sun and Rane *from the skies . . .*

        is nigh, or is it *night?*

31

love given taken (my love my) work
for the night for the days

that are left— trans-
parent iris pale blue sky open

into day broken

open into night

OUT OF DOORS

OUT OF DOORS

August 2012

1

Out of doors, outdoors
In summer we play . . .

out of, as in ingredients

wouldn't go to the beach without

Doors? We are all out

2

out of, as in immigrants

out, as in no vote

Last night we ran against
each other, rage ran

against rage, voted No

3

No way back

to last week's beach,
seals: one Gothic
head raised, others long
black buttons . . .

to God, unbuttoning

4

Buttons rolling, toys
on wheels, dozens

of sandpipers, notes,
allegro, eighths, Bach
in the sand, cannot

read this restless score

5

Score unsettled: he
imagined someone else, I
screamed *You . . . you . . . you . . .*

But there is something
else (smudged

now): there is this

6

This: not the dragon-
fly plucking watery

thoughts, or the greeny sun-
fish under, but these grass-

thin lines writing back,
answering, holding

7

Holding off those want-
one-too's, it's *our* bomb we got it
first, used twice this week back then

These days, it's war waged from a box
then home to dinner, kids, TV—

Flag: if it were just for these medaled runners

8

Run along now, out of my—

house to house to hut
to hut to tent to home

from school from work to— Rage

exploding on streets   Rage in my house

9

House on city street
again with *tree* house *tree*
house in lines: no winding road—

with rows of roses, tubs of sun-
flowers, shrubs, cosmos
fenced: no meadow, sea

10

See the locust making her flowers
green confetti, as May made

her pink, her apple white—

See the apples, see the dark apples

of the eyes of our late storm

11

Storms, flooding, fires
raging, soil cracking, prices
rising, heat, our hottest year—

Rage against polluters, deniers,
don't-care-about prosperers—

Here, in my tiny life, cool, forgive

12

For-give once meant give
or give up or give
in marriage, as in bride—

But I was not
given: chose my own,
gave myself— though not

completely, as in *for-*

13

For night is coming, we
will be done, fight's a way to deny—

In the labyrinth, turning, I saw
myself in the mirror, recalled
of God in us, thought *in me*

Then, still, small: *There is more*

14

More to do: *Play God,* as in
imitate, said the minister—

Out of all my doors
into the room
all of God could be, all

room, as in space, without doors

15

Doors open: front
side and back: summer come in

But ending's begun: apricot-
colored leaves on the ground, bits
of fruit-like yellow high in the birch—

the old, the article said, and *the old old*

16

Old tree, house, town, old
story, plot, all told—

Forget the green purse lost
in the dream, the bad connection

A big tree, he said, my first
visit, *you can't miss*

17

Missing the under- :

the touched licked
tongued linked the

buttons all over that body—

wanting that wanting

18

Wanting the lilac, flute
that April, pond, canoe
that July, the getting to know

before the gotten to, getting
on, before this still don't know

each other, dark beside dark

19

Dark lake mirrors gray clouds
where I walk toward dawn, behind
me black gloss mirroring trees—

Under us, maybe, dark, not
over us shining, but deep in the—

. . . *made darkness His secret place*

20

Place of childhood summers:
lake, pines, cabins, family: five

daughters of three sisters, two
born in this month (I said
I'd put that in), all born

out of those tiny bodies of water

21

Water pinks, blues, geese
stretch, ducks stir, green heron
rises, slow, up to the dock—

as last month's great blue, wings
over me, in the water, came

down, like the come-down Dove

22

Mourning dove in the morning,
geese, gulls working all day—

until sun, gold through silvered
clouds, through rose, rests

for a moment, then slips
into the slot between water and sky

23

Sky bled from sun's cut

a short sentence

How many years do you get?

Tombstones in the corner
of the dream: SMALL and AUGUST

24

August going: summer homes
shuttered, ghost-wrapped boat

Queen Anne's lace
curled in, crickets, grass-
hoppers up from my path

Storm door goes in, screen out

25

out of my _____ just
woke up what _____

about the _____ what _____
at the _____ just my _____

place of _____ memory lost
most of this day

26

Day the next: loss moved on,
transient, pack on its back

Back to mind as known, as
in intimate, not a stranger

But not long until loss
moves in to stay

27

Stay, Love, beside me in
our bed again, on the sometimes
rocky path through still green woods

Meant to think *spirit* again, got *brain*
this time, matter, neurons, *Save*—

unpleated days hanging from my lines

28

Lines outside, books in: school
days, but for us it's night

unto night, adding up

Still day tonight, the late sun—

Just a word, Love, a few letters

29

Letter erased, beginning
with date, name the last to go

Then off the lost
track to the closing door
marked *Way back home*—

Only the writing on the bones

30

Bones found, bodies, bombs,
doors smashed, doors

shut in their, cannot
vote for their any—

Night pours in, they
are poured out like water

31

Water scribes the sand,
the floor of the water, sky blues

the water, glosses the sand, sand
mirrors the evening light, waves

slate the sand for night
to write its one last word

DRAWN IN

DRAWN IN

February 2013

1

Out of the pool, into her small
        water, out of the water in
                to the picture, drawn

in, bodied and faced
        for now for now is how
                we are, our small our

2

Ours, before us, over the big
        water I've crossed back over,

                others centuries before
on these stone streets, shaped
        by these hills, held by these walls

                of this for now my small city

3

City where Catherine
 and Jesus traded hearts

   as in the paintings: *He*
makes of her another Himself—

  Incarnate: God in self,
    neighbor— God inside out

4

Outside the city, an unbroken
  wall with fourteen towers:
    Dante's model for giants

   around the Abyss, around
  this tiny town with gardens: what
shall walls keep out, keep in?

5

Kept in, in my own country, for
        little, for less, for life: our

                war on crime's on, white
over black, as in this city's emblem:

        colors here for horses that run,
                not for people who can't

6

can see, over the walls of brick
        and stone, crests of hills, points
                of cypress, can look

                through stone arches, arches
        beside and beyond arches—
to go out is to go through

7

Through my window, tile roofs
    with chimneys with pillars
        and roofs: houses as if

for the pigeons, or for the starlings
    patterning sheets of sky, drawing

        in the blue that roofs the world

8

World without end, though in
    the paintings it's all ends:
        birth then death—

Beginning, the end of Epiphany,
    ending soon, Word . . .

        Gold, in the paintings. God.

9

God of confetti, costumes, kids
      as princess, Superman, duck—

          God of *Carnivale*, of our having,
then of our giving up, our not—

      God of the ashes of and to which
          we are sorry ashes we are

10

. . . are as gnarled gray arms
      that are winter's vineyards, skins
          of grapes in a mound—

or the ever-green leaves
      of the olive, their under-
          sides gray, silvered by sun—

11

Sun lighting—*instead of a field,*
    a house, a stream, a movement
       of clouds—

landscape, which didn't exist

    until the eyes of an artist drew
      it all together

12

Gathering days, as clouds
    in a darkening sky, or scraps

      of days: gleaning what
is left before the night when more
    than stars— when dark

    comes out and we come in

13

In time, the bells call, time
    for ashes *mea culpa* small

      I spilt broke bent
hurt did not care and not

      to care did— oh there is *mea culpa* no
        could have I cannot own

14

him my own one
    sweet heart hum
        of love you are my sun

        sometimes moon
    that curves my small
I into a heart

15

Green heart of the country, blood
    of sunrise over the hills,

            while in the valley
jewels of light, and near us trees

        coming out for the day and here

            it is: *Itself the Sun*

16

Sun leaving, taking the sheep
        that filled the morning road, now
            the road, the distant trees, taking

            these closer leaves, branches, now
        these trees, taking the valley (but now
those lights—!) taking the hills

17

Hills, one dressed in brown-
    green trees, the other bared
        for houses that own it, dots

of olive trees smocking the green
    beneath, and a ribbon

        of road drawing me in

18

In again through the gate
    to the city, sienna gold ochre
        gray, palette of brick

and stone, past the grand piazza
    where horses in summer . . . and down

        my narrow street where, small, I am

19

Am I drawing on, in this not-
      my-city, or drawing over, child
         with a crayon on thin

paper, when I am wanting
      to draw in, into another
         picture, its thick layers?

20

Layers of stone and we add
      our dead, our junk, to the top—

         where Dante, knowing
nothing of crust or core, made his own
      layers down, where he had

      to go, on his way, down

21

Down the drones bombs out
    the guns money's muck buy

       here as there then

as now we *other* city country
    immigrant, can we with no
       them with only *our* . . .

22

Ourselves, all of us, *God*
    only through neighbors,

       said Catherine, *Can*
we all . . . said that man

       they beat: *one another*, the all
         who die who are ourselves

23

Our selves, him and mine, my
        him is here, I'd forgotten

                how very . . . Oh Love, even
this can turn hurt (that torn-

        up girl—) But you're here, un-
                hurt, unhurting you

24

You: not my other
        half better something gold
                as in the paintings, you

                do not make of me another
        you, we are two, but more
than one and one, oh Love—

25

Love, wrote Catherine, my mother
    Katheryn, Dante, that mountain

      with snow, this snow-
slushed rain: no rose but a going

    toward (the paintings' risings, raised
    hands) from *You Are Here*

26

News from hundreds of years ago: GALILEO
    CONFINED, BANK [now world's oldest] OPENS,
      CATHERINE GOES TO AVIGNON TO GET POPE—

And from this month: [the same] BANK
    BAILED OUT, POPE RESIGNS, NO WINNER
    IN THIS ELECTION—no one in

27

In sight—as at the bottom of this narrow
        street the church—comes the end

                of this small month, and where
has it led? In, on, past, back

        with my love again, bells

                ringing, morning drawing us in

28

In this little time left, time
        to go, time for once

                more into this past of brick
and stone, layered with late and later now:

        For now, *Grazie, tutti*, I am almost
                at the gate, I'm going through

Siena, Italy

IN TIME

IN TIME

June 2014

1

A day they said   my mother just
mayfly life   rush fly drive ten
years ago through just-

greened trees bleeding
hearts by the door to the door

to her last   bed   days   just

in time   a minute beside   her then

2

Beside her bed not one
day but eight I sang and she
kept time:
              songs she wrote, one
for Jesus, one for . . .

Juno's month or children's
month (see Ovid)   mother's / mine

(have I fallen into   her life . . .

3

Fallen into my own
now but then deep
into her:
              days with nothing
between   out of myself   let
myself go before *she*

let go   went gone   into the blue

out of this world   eyes   sky

4

Out of the book
of yesterday:
                one with her
name   another   a river
I swam against the current

pages I hadn't turned
for years   back until my then
body self's   my own now

5

My own she said but who
was whose?
                  chirp chirp
chirp against the traffic

Her last word
was *no* but then a nod
when the minister prayed *give*

us this day   that last day

6

was late that day
of departure but in time

to shut her eyes touch her still
warm hands that once

played Chopin   planted
beside our house the white

and blue that were her garden

7

Blue the delphinium
iris   climbing clematis
rising each June—
                    Herbarium
blues the year before I was born:
forget-me-not   meadow rue
heal-all   speedwell

and *pearly everlasting*

8

My pearl   she said   *forever*
she   to me   *no one else's*

Pink blossoms coming
and going:
                    peonies fluttering
open   rhododendron
dropping their tiny skirts:

she   pink she   body abloom

9

She: body open for all
the world . . . for one . . .

Later spoke in tongues
once, as on this day: little
tongues of fire spirit come down

to raise up   heavenly dove—

tongue body bodies   and then tongues

10

And then blood   that red day
spirit poured out   moon into blood

Her *pearl of great price*, she said:

from *kingdom of heaven?* or was it
that other red-letter book she read?

Song written for one become
song sung for Another

11

Songs all sung   red
in the garden   a fence

around it she said   roses
on every fence but now

must shut the gate

—while over the border
the houses   towns . . .

12

The house where we lived

Friends in the house

A book being written

A bird in the house

A doctor calling for someone else

Sparrow flying up the stairs

Fly, little bird, up and across the sky

13

Mouthed across the room *long*
evening became *longing* no
longing became—

mused across the long lines

missed across the miles not—

(wanting was what I wanted)

not missed out on   not to be missed

14

Out on the streets   out of
a country: new army old
war new flag old

blood   guns   rush
of multitudes fleeing

or falling   on their

own shadows   under them now

15

Shadows (shades) under, angels
over, and we between: flush
of love   gush

of hands fingers severed
bodies stoned shot
into graves
                    while we without
blood on our   could   if we   do

16

The bloodless ones: her fattening
pistil, his feathery anthers
(peony poppy) at work
over spread petals

Or a robin fallen out of its nest—
no a fledgling off the ground then
down-and-back-under-the-fence

17

Under the tangle of all
these startings stoppings long-
ings mutterings:
                    good
the minister said *and it
was good—*
                    or is it just
reaching toward least-ness
into not-ness   or just   in time?

18

Body in time with body
my one my love will be
beside me again   was
has again is—
                    could also
mention the breeze swaying
the trees   green dance now

that wanting is what I have

19

what I have is what is so rare

as this more than day our daily our more

than breath this birdsong hum

of machine of something sirens more

than this music of what is so how

am I why to deserve

this more than I ever had?

20

Not more but other, a second
shift: dahlias daisies day-
lilies taking over—
                    or same
but over again, like the robins'
second mating—
                    while I should be
on my way, like those roses about
to go, but
                    not yet not yet not yet

21

to go without a   where   to
pack   without an *in*   vanish
under so   much blue

along this longest day to
draw the line where body

stops   slips   some
time on the way   back home

22

On the tree outside this smudged
window tiny apples bulge
between flower and stem

In the garden the snake did not
lie: they *did*, as promised, know—

did eat touch what had been
there all the time   hidden inside

23

On a hidden sandbar a gull
walks as if on water, two
gulls now, one flying up
then back
         . . . less
sandbar now but still gull
standing as if—
              gull and one
cormorant diving under

24

Diving under   in   *cannot*
not I thought   and deeply
did   am
         —catbird gray
on the rocks beside
my walk   walks *with*

me now   shadow to my
can better for my   do

25

To do today: dog walking
me straight into summer
no swerve no time like . . .

heat also inside come
from between when there's no
between as in air and body

or body and body

26

and body will fail   my friend
today his brain   my love
his missing . . .
                in time all
will turn (sandbar under
again) all parts—
                    for now body
and body   sweet sweat
a wet   (for)getting

27

Forgot the weeds   the pullings
and diggings   this month of black
swallowwort taking the garden
claiming the fence—
                          forgot
the black clouds   warnings
storms   forgot the days of
It's really coming down!

28

Often forget what's coming these long
days I meant to be thinking *night*
unto night—
                    But now
my friend his pressured
brain   and my love . . .
                              Death holds life
on a short leash, but oh when romping

o breaks free from no—

29

Free from then-past and then-
to-come for moments

of love that measures time
by what it makes that makes

time stop or seem . . .

is the bed where we lie . . .

this in   just in time

30

Awake in time   for this red
blaze behind trees:
                    different
window bed house but
my own one beside me all
well for now
                    my little only
life my own to take out

of night into this   given day

LEAVING BEHIND

LEAVING BEHIND

November 2015

1

Open up for close
out   soul-clothes   every-
thing has to go   closing

down time   call them all
saints   souls   my own gone

ones: Andy   Marcia   Mary Alice
Mary Anne   cloud of all   carried out

2

outside my window: locust, cloth
of gold   on the ground: its yellow

tabs   linden hearts   sweet gum stars
like cutouts from the same . . .

paper-napkin ghosts fill a tree near
the house where a year ago my friend—

rust-colored chrysanthemums   rust-colored door

3

door to door the angel no the Lord
passed or did not pass—

the angel opened the prison
door   doors to pass through, out
or in: our millions, more than any—

in the other story the Lord
said: *to put a difference between*

4

between one and another
a gun: at one end it's a good

gun because at the other's a cell
phone pill bottle toy gun nothing a

Trayvon   Tamir   Dontre   Michael
Laquan   Eric   Rekia   John: call

them out and the others, Black and many

5

many thousand gone   no
more auction block   slaves gone

up north where I am going
again, coppery oak leaves holding
on, overlaid with gold, then just rust
above the skeletal gray . . .

chains gone, or gone before, more—

6

more new neighbors residing
on these avenues: thousands in white
marble: WHITMAN HARVEY HARRIS BLISS—

past yellowing birch and weeping beech
at the intersection of Larch and Oak
WHITNEY SPENCER JEWELL: a startle

of Japanese maple spreading red

7

red shadow on pale
moon: earth curtain

drawn slowly across
quarter half almost

across: weeks ago, weeks

of my small life, child-

sized life so little left

8

left them there
FATHER   MOTHER
left, leaving their living—

their death-days:
his Labor, her June

yellow circles of leaves beneath—

something left behind

9

behind all that is
is not   God: still, small
silence of   not beyond
beneath before but

no   where   name

blue sky gray

cloud that is   not there

10

There was a road, long,
gray, with a dotted line—

wanted to write
old, I thought years ago
young, and here it is: road

running out, gold gone
now, cut here   cut to old

11

old vets: in 2012 the last
from the First, Great, the war
to end all wars, its Armistice honored
the cause of world peace but there was

the Second, not even a million left and now
it's *all* Veterans—suicides, homeless, parades
rained on today, our post-traumatic war

12

wars now, TEN TO WATCH: Syria/Isis
Ukraine S.Sudan Nigeria Congo Afghanistan

while the faithful debate: *turn the other* or
uniformed Christ with rifle, as in the First—

while boys spill toy soldiers, khaki and green
with tanks and guns, from a plastic tub—

while leaves dry to khaki on our ground

13

ground covered with oak leaves, crisp
and tan, and others under, crushed
into brown, soon to be earth—

but sun still lighting the threadleaf
Japanese maples apricot plum

sun still paling my pink-tinged skin
blood showing through my thinned

14

thinned to spindly twigs with dangles
of pods the once-gold locust—

thinner the ice and higher the seas
and hotter the planet and what will be done
at the Paris talks to slow it   Paris

where last night terrorists killed and Beirut—

to stop the killing the dying earth   to turn

15

turn on red   stop
light to go   light

touch   blood   love
light   wrote mind-

field for   mine-   it's
a gold   mine   rising

into light   field to go

16

go with me, my love, my one
into that night where one will go

before the other but still our night
boat our bed   our lovers' tongues
songs in the night   nor the moon

by night   our little light   night-

night my love   by and by

17

by order of   no exit except

the angel troubled the pool but

stubble before the wind just

two apples left on this tree—

cloud from *clūd*, rock, but

the stars we see are not stars but

light   but cloud over light

18

lights out wars on last
days end-times reckoning left

behind but which us them not one
stone upon another nation against

mirror terror Jesus Isa no one knows but
hurry it up faster let climate also be

a sign   beginning of sorrows

19

sorrow sorrow my friend's last bed

just five months after they said he . . .

behind the rust-colored door

brown brown all leaves on the ground

requiem aeternam we sang together

year years all tumbled down

et lux perpetua   light

20

light of sun on sweet gum leaves
glisten of amber and green or

sudden light of gunfire, bombs:
Nigeria now (two girls, one
eleven, strapped into suicide
vests) and Mali: the world

lit with the light of darkness

21

darkness He called . . . or darkness
we make, denying the fallen among,
the recent threatened tortured escaped:

send them back send them to camps
make them register carry ID's
close down their mosques let only

Christians   passing by on the other

22

other, the once-red Japanese
maple, bare now, gray but

see its great muscled limbs
stretch out low, then curve up

as if to embrace, climb on a limb
and see in the cleft a small cluster,

as if arranged, of curling red

23

red heart pulse of—

red the fountain filled
with Jesus' blood, in another
country filled with martyrs'—

red the last apple on the tree I
could reach if I leaned—

red that looks blue until it's shed

24

shed skin feathers leaves water
-shed dividing line deciding

time   earth-age named
anthro- for us, our own doing our
undoing losing dying unless—

the most fit the worst
fit for earth in all its ages

25

age mine day mine past
my appointed   night

mine   full moon   mourning
moon in an old sky   light:

wanted to make an opening
out of closing down but

enough to leave behind

26

behind them a mighty ocean
around them *beasts and wilde men*

after them us, closing our shores

ahead of us, rising oceans

forgive us this day our
immigrant past that isn't even—

first which shall be last

27

last chance ditch effort gasp:

gone-before last and could-be last:
how much can one elegy hold?

could this be it? a friend wrote, her last
words— last lost *it* for all our earth?

but last night that moon, all the way home

—from Old English *follow:*   to last beyond last

28

last night I woke and found my body-
held living-for-now a piece of all—

over the graves the beautiful
skeletal: chalice and vase, tangle
and dance, the white bones
of the birch, its vertical script—

over my bones, this living that is my

29

my life my living my being my loving

my friend my friends my one my love

the huge white moon, missing almost nothing

my love in my arms, in my bed again

the advent candle for earth for hope

this almost last this work these leavings

my blessings my many my thanks for these

30

these days and nights, these lines
have changed (*you must change*)
my life my loving (my one) and

now this leaving behind this opening

out (the spaces between the dark
lines of the great unleaved) to where

the night is as clear as the day

NOTES AND ACKNOWLEDGMENTS

"Up North": The poem was written in Ithaca, New York, during a semester in which three Cornell students committed suicide by jumping from bridges into gorges that run through the campus.

"Broken Open": The first section describes a May Day custom of my childhood; the second references attempts by Congress to dissociate American May Day from the Communist holiday. Osama bin Laden was killed on May 2, 2011, a fact referenced in 4, which includes some words of Dr. Martin Luther King, Jr. (by way of Jim Wallace); 28 references Pascal. The last line in 30 (Memorial Day) is indebted to a prose poem by Lili Glauber which refers to her misunderstanding of the last line of "Taps" when she was a child. "Broken Open" is in memory of Joseph DeRoche (1938–2013), my muse for this poem.

"Out of Doors": The first "week" of this poem coincided with the second week of the 2012 Summer Olympics. At the end of the month, I experienced a weird but predictably short episode of transient global amnesia.

"Drawn In": Except for a brief excursion into Umbria, this poem was written in Siena, Italy, famous for its summer horse race, the *Palio*, and for Saint Catherine of Siena, who is referred to throughout. The italicized line and complete thought in 11 are from Georg Simmel (1858–1918).

"In Time": Section 9 references Pentecost, which celebrates the descent of the Holy Spirit on the apostles, as portrayed in the New Testament book of Acts. For the "pearl of great price" in 10, see Matthew 13:46.

"Leaving Behind": The poem opens on All Saints' Day, and occasionally references, explicitly and implicitly, the Paris Climate Change Conference (November 30–December 11, 2015). Section 18 references Mark 13:2-8, as well as Islamic predictions of the end-times (Isa is the Muslim name for Jesus). The quoted words in 26 are from a 1620 record of the Plymouth Colony, based on the account of William Bradford.

My deep gratitude to Cornell University, for support during spring 2010, when "Up North" was written; to the Siena Art Institute, for a fellowship during February 2013, when "Drawn In" was written; and to the Radcliffe Institute for Advanced Study, for its support of 40 Concord Avenue, where many sections of the other poems were written.

"Up North" first appeared in *Plume*, "Broken Open" in *Poet Lore*, "Drawn In" in the *Cincinnati Review*, "Out of Doors" in the *New England Review*, "In Time" in *Salamander*, and "Leaving Behind" in *Poetry*. My thanks to the editors of these publications.

Doug Macomber

MARTHA COLLINS is the author of nine volumes of poetry, including *Admit One: An American Scrapbook* and *Day Unto Day*. She has also published four collections of cotranslated Vietnamese poetry, including *Black Stars: Poems by Ngo Tu Lap* (with the author). Her awards include fellowships from the NEA, the Bunting Institute, and the Witter Bynner Foundation, as well as an Anisfield-Wolf Award, two Ohioana Awards, the Laurence Goldstein Poetry Prize, and three Pushcart Prizes. Founder of the creative writing program at UMass-Boston, she served as Pauline Delaney Professor of Creative Writing at Oberlin College until 2007, and is currently editor-at-large for *FIELD* magazine and one of the editors of the Oberlin College Press.

milkweed
editions

Founded as a nonprofit organization in 1980, Milkweed Editions is an independent publisher. Our mission is to identify, nurture and publish transformative literature, and build an engaged community around it.

milkweed.org

Interior design based on a design
by Gretchen Achilles / Wavetrap Design
Typeset in Dante
by Mary Austin Speaker

Dante is a midcentury typeface designed by Giovanni Mardersteig
for the Officina Bodoni, and its design was influenced by types cut
by Francesco Griffo in the late fifteenth or early sixteenth century.
Dante was named for the book in which it was first
used—Boccaccio's *Tratello in Laude di Dante*, or
Little Treatise in Praise of Dante.